Public Speaking for Kids

Activity and Coloring Book

Grades K-5

Fundamentals of Public Speaking and Types of Speeches

Copyright, 2020
ISBN – 978-1-7352138-0-4
Written, Designed and Illustrated by Jessieca Montgomery Riley
Public Speaking and Leadership Skills for Kids in grades K-5
Printed in the United States of America

This book is dedicated to
All the gifted, talented and bold young public speakers
in the world!

This book belongs to:

Fundamentals of Public Speaking

What is Public Speaking?

LaKeisha

Who is Your Public?

Judah   Joseph

LeRoi   Esther

Larry   Rachel

Lisa

Judah   Joseph

LeRoi   Esther

Everyone.

Leah   Peter

What is Projection?

Larry

What is Eye Contact?

Peter

When you look at someone's eyes the same time
they look at yours.

Is Eye Contact important? Why?

Esther

What are Filler Words?

LeRoi

Words we use to fill in for other words.

Example: Um, Ahh, Uhh

Don't forget to Smile!

Rachel

It will make your audience feel welcome.

It's okay to be nervous.

Joseph

Always practice before giving a speech.

Jacob

Yes! Practice, practice, practice.

Watch your Pacing?

Judah

What is a Lectern?

Public Speaking
for Kids!

You stand behind it when delivering
a speech.

Types of Speeches

Demonstrative

Peter

Informative

Abraham

Descriptive

Lisa

Helps the audience to understand a process by hearing a description.

Persuasive
(per-sway-siv)

Larry

Sharing your ideas and convincing your audience to agree with you.

Entertaining

Rachel

Motivational

LeRoi

Includes words that inspire your audience to do things that makes them happy.

Impromptu
(m-promp-2)

Esther

Special Occasion

Joseph

A short speech used to introduce a someone or something.

Debate

Leah

Sharing your ideas and explaining why you think they are the best.

Create your own type of speech!

Jacob

Let's write a speech!
Notes for your public speaker

Leah

Speech Preparation:

If your speaker is still learning to read and write full sentences, encourage them to draw a picture of their speech.

- Allow 15 min to draw or write speech
- Give a two-minute warning
- Begin countdown at 10 seconds
- Time is up!

Speech Delivery:

Do:
- Confirm the speaker is ready
- Ask speaker to stand (behind a lectern, if available)
- Encourage speaker by applauding and cheering loudly
- Remind speaker to smile and breathe
- Confirm the speaker is ready again
- Start the timer
- Laugh with the speaker, not at them
- Let the time run out. Allow the alarm to sound.

Don't:
- Allow the speaker to watch the timer
- Inform the speaker of how much time they have left to speak.
- Laugh at the speaker.
- Allow speaker to put hands in their pockets or fidget
- Distract the speaker by moving, texting or talking

Have fun!

Let's write a speech!

Esther

Suggested picture layout for drawn speeches:

"Awesome Introduction" – Draw Picture Here	"Mighty Middle" – Draw Picture Here	"Excellent Ending" – Draw Picture Here

Let's write a speech!
Warm-Up Speech

Jacob

Warm-up Speech: "I like to (add name here)"
Time: 10 Seconds
Supplies: Timer, crayons, pencil, paper and creativity

Speech Prompt:

"Hello, my name is _____ and
                    (First Name)

I like to _____ because _____.

Thank you! (stop timer here)

Start timer when the speaker is ready. Presenters who
are not yet reading or writing in full sentences, can draw
a picture and describe what is in their picture within 10
seconds.

Speakers should always face their audience when
presenting.

Speech Time:

1st Try: _____

2nd Try: _____

3rd Try: _____

Reward your speaker with encouragement and applause.

Let's write a speech!
Descriptive

Topic: Describe your favorite place to visit
Time: 1:00 Minute
Supplies: Timer, crayons, pencil, paper and creativity

Speech Prompt:

Awesome Introduction

"Hello, my name is (First Name)_____ and I will

describe my favorite place to visit in four words.

Mighty Middle (body)

"It is _____, _____, _____ and

_____". If I were there now, I

would _____. That is why it is my favorite

place to visit.

Excellent Ending (conclusion)

"Can you guess my favorite place to visit? Thank you! (stop timer here)

Start timer when the speaker is ready. Presenters who are not yet reading or writing in full sentences, can draw a picture and describe what is in their picture within 1 minute.

Speakers should always face their audience when presenting.

Speech Time:

1st Try: _____

2nd Try: _____

3rd Try: _____

Reward your speaker with encouragement and applause. Peter

Let's write a speech!
Demonstrative

Topic: Demonstrate how to make a <u>(your title here)</u>.
Time: 2:00 Minute
Supplies: Timer, crayons, pencil, paper and creativity

<u>Speech Prompt:</u>

<u>Awesome Introduction</u>

"Hello, my name is _____ and I will demonstrate
                    (First Name)

how to make a _____ in four steps."

<u>Mighty Middle (body)</u>

"Step 1_____. Step 2 _____. Step 3_____

_____. Step 4_____."

<u>Excellent Ending (conclusion)</u>

"And that is how you make a _____ " Thank you! (stop timer here)

Start timer when the speaker is ready. Presenters who are not yet reading or writing in full sentences, can draw a picture and describe what is in their picture within 1 minute.

Speakers should always face their audience when presenting.

<u>Speech Time:</u>

1st Try: _____

2nd Try: _____

3rd Try: _____

Rachel

Reward your speaker with encouragement and applause.

Let's write a speech!

Topic: _____

Time: 10 sec.

_____

_____

_____

_____

_____

_____

_____

_____

_____

_____

_____

Let's write a speech!

Topic: _____

Time: <u>1 Min.</u>

_____

_____

_____

_____

_____

_____

_____

_____

_____

_____

Let's write a speech!

Topic: _____

Time: <u>2 Min.</u>

_____

_____

_____

_____

_____

_____

_____

_____

_____

_____

Let's write a speech!

Topic: _____

Time: _____

_____

_____

_____

_____

_____

_____

_____

_____

_____

_____

_____

Let's write a speech!

Topic: _____

Time: _____

_____

_____

_____

_____

_____

_____

_____

_____

_____

_____

Let's write a speech!

Topic: _____

Time: _____

_____

_____

_____

_____

_____

_____

_____

_____

_____

_____

Types of Speeches

Debate

Persuasive

Descriptive

Demonstrative

Impromptu

Informative

Special Occasion

Entertaining

References

Team, C. (n.d.). *Clippings.me*. Retrieved from https://www.clippings.me/blog/types-of-speeches/

Happy Speaking!
It's a good thing!

Thank you!

Thank you for purchasing our books. It takes a lot of courage to face the challenges of being shy, butterflies in the belly and crazy nerves. We are very proud of you and your speaker!

Keep up the good work and Happy Speaking!

Speak EZ for Kids Books

"Fundamentals of Public Speaking
and Timing"

"Fundamentals of Public Speaking and
Types of Speeches"

"Fundamentals of Public Speaking, Sounds and Words We
Choose"

Negative Thoughts Journals
"Negative Thoughts Go in Here! That's It!"
"Negative Thoughts Go in Here! That's It! For Girls"
"Negative Thoughts Go in Here! That's It!
For Youths"

Contact us
SpeakEZ for Kids
PO Box 2011, Waldorf, MD 20601
speakezforkids@gmail.com
www.speakezforkds.com